The Story of Hanukkah

The Story of
Hanukkah

GRAMERCY BOOKS
• New York •

This 1997 edition is published by Gramercy Books,
a division of Random House Value Publishing, Inc.,
201 East 50th Street, New York, New York 10022.

Gramercy Books and colophon are trademarks of
Random House Value Publishing, Inc.

Random House
New York • Toronto • London • Sydney • Auckland

Printed and bound in China

Compiled, edited, designed, and composited by
Frank J. Finamore

A CIP catalog record for this book is available from the
Library of Congress.

The Story of Hanukkah
ISBN 0–517–18360–9

8   7   6   5   4   3   2

✡ CONTENTS ✡

The Hanukkah Celebration

Hanukkah Recipes

✡ PREFACE ✡

Hanukkah, or the Festival of Lights, celebrates the revolt and victory of Jewish
forces led by Judah Maccabee and his brothers—sons of Mattathias the Priest, members of
the Hasmonean family—over King Antiochus IV
and the Syrian-Greeks; it is a celebration of the
reestablishment of Jewish independence.

The Jews of Palestine rebelled under
Antiochus' oppressive rule. He turned the Temple
in Jerusalem into a pagan shrine and attempted
to force the Jews to abandon the worship of their
religion by outlawing circumcision and the study
of the Torah.

The central event that Hanukkah celebrates is
the rededication and cleansing of the Temple on
the twenty-fifth of the month of Kislev in 165
B.C.E. after the Syrian-Greeks were driven out of
Jerusalem. The word *Hanukkah* in Hebrew
means rededication.

The story of Judah Maccabee and the Jewish

revolt is recounted in the Book of Maccabees, which is a part of the *Apocrypha,* books which are not part of the *Tanach,* or Holy Scriptures. The rabbis who compiled the scriptures did not think the story of Judah and the restoration of the monarchy under the Hasmoneans important enough for inclusion into the Biblical canon, as Jewish tradition maintained that the only true kingship of Israel could be held by a member of the House of David, descendants of the tribe of Judah, which the Hasmonean family was not.

Hanukkah is always celebrated on the twenty-fifth of Kislev on the Jewish calendar, which is based on solar and lunar factors. The date differs each year on the standard Roman calendar because in Jewish leap years an extra month is added and changes significantly the date of the holiday.

For much of the last two thousand years, Hanukkah has been considered a minor holiday, but following World War II, it has grown in popularity and importance. Even in America, it is more than a Jewish answer to Christmas. With the rebirth of the state of Israel, Hanukkah celebrates the heroic resolve of the Jewish spirit and its eternal faith in God.

NATHAN GREEN

New York
1997

From

The First
Book of
Maccabees

Chapter 1

And it happened, after that Alexander, son of Philip, the Macedonian, who came out of the land of Chettiim, had defeated Darius, king of the Persians and Medes, that he reigned in his stead, first over Greece, and made many wars, and won many strongholds, and slew the kings of the earth, and went through to the ends of the earth, and took spoils of many nations, inasmuch that the earth was quiet before him; whereupon he was exalted, and his heart was lifted up. And he gathered a mighty strong army, and ruled over countries, and nations, and kings, who became tributaries unto him. And after these things he fell sick, and perceived that he should die. Wherefore he called his servants, such as were honorable, and had been brought up with him from his youth, and parted his kingdom among them, while he was yet alive. So Alexander reigned twelve years, and then died. And then his officers ruled in his place. And after his death they all put crowns upon themselves and so did their descendants after them many years: and evils were multiplied in the earth.

And there came out of them a wicked root, Antiochus surnamed Epiphanes, son of Antiochus the king, who had been a hostage in Rome, and he reigned in the hundred and thirty-seventh year of the kingdom of the Greeks.

In those days went there out of Israel wicked men, who persuaded many, saying, "Let us go and make a covenant with the Gentiles that are round about us, for since we departed from them we have had much sorrow." So this device pleased them well. Then certain of the people were so forward herein, that they went to the king, who gave them license to do after the ordinances of the Gentiles. So they built a place of exercise in Jerusalem according to the customs of the Gentiles, and made themselves uncircumcised, forsook the holy covenant. They joined themselves to the Gentiles and sold themselves to evil.

Now after Antiochus established his rule over the kingdom, he thought to reign over Egypt, that he might have the dominion of two realms. Wherefore he entered into Egypt with a great multitude—with chariots, elephants, horsemen, and a great navy— and made war against Ptolemy king of Egypt. But Ptolemy was afraid of him and fled, and many were killed. They captured the strong cities in the land of Egypt and plundered the land.

And after Antiochus defeated Egypt, he returned again in the hundred forty-third year, and went up against Israel and Jerusalem with a great force, and entered arrogantly into the sanctuary, and took away the golden altar, the candlesticks, and all the utensils. He took also the table for bread offerings, the cups, the bowls, the censers of gold, the curtain, the crowns, and the golden ornaments that were before the temple—all of which he stripped off. He took also the silver and the gold, and the precious vessels, as well as the hidden treasures which he found. And when he had taken all away, he went into his own land, after committing a great massacre of which he spoke with arrogant boasting. Therefore there was great mourning in Israel, in every place where they were; so that the princes and elders mourned, the virgins and young men were made feeble, and the beauty of women was changed. Every bridegroom took up lamentation, and she that sat in the marriage chamber was in heaviness. The land also was moved for the inhabitants and all the house of Jacob were covered with confusion.

Two years later the king sent his chief collector of tribute to the cities of Judaea, and he came to Jerusalem with a strong force, and spoke peaceable words to them, but all was deceit. When they believed his lies, he suddenly fell upon the city, and smote it very sore, destroying many people of Israel. He plundered the city and set it on fire, and pulled down the houses and walls on every side. They took the women and children captive, and took the cattle. Then they built around the city of David a great and strong wall with mighty towers and made it a stronghold for them. And they put therein a sinful nation, wicked men, and fortified themselves therein. They stored it with arms and supplies, and when they had gathered together the spoils of Jerusalem, they laid them up there, and so they became a sore snare; for it was a place to lie in wait against the sanctuary and an evil adversary to Israel. Thus they shed innocent blood on every side of the sanctuary, and defiled it, inasmuch that the inhabitants of Jerusalem fled because of them; whereupon the city was made an habitation of strangers, and became strange to those that were born in her and her own children left her. Her sanctuary was laid waste like a wilderness, her feasts were turned into mourning, her sabbaths into reproach, her honor into contempt. As had been her glory, so was her dishonor increased, and her excellency was turned into mourning.

Moreover King Antiochus wrote to his whole kingdom, that all should be one people, and everyone should give up their customs. The Gentiles agreed according to the commandment of the King. Yea, many also of the Israelites consented to his religion, and sacrificed to idols, and profaned the Sabbath. For the king had sent letters by messengers to Jerusalem and the cities of Judaea, that they should follow the strange laws of the land, to forbid burnt offerings, sacrifices and drink offerings in the temple; to profane the Sabbaths and festival days; to defile the sanctuary and holy people; to set up altars and groves and chapels for idols; to sacrifice swine flesh and unclean beasts; to leave their children uncircumcised. They were to make their souls abominable with all manner of uncleanness and profanation so in the end they would forget the law, and change all the ordinances. And whosoever would not do according to the commandment of the king would die.

In the selfsame manner the king wrote to his whole kingdom and appointed overseers over all the people, commanding the cities of Judaea to sacrifice, city by city. Then many of the people were gathered unto them—everyone that forsook the law—and so they committed evils in the land and drove the Israelites into hiding in every place of refuge they had.

Now the fifteenth day of the month Kislev, in the hundred forty-fifth year, they set up the abomination of desolation upon the altar, and built idol altars throughout the cities of Judaea on every side; and burnt incense at the doors of their houses, and in the streets. And when they had rent in pieces the books of the law they found, they burnt them with fire. And whoever was found with any the book of the testament, or if any consented to the law, the king's commandment was, that they should put him to death. Thus did they, by their authority, to the Israelites every month, to as many as were found in the cities. On the twenty-fifth day of the month they did sacrifice upon the idol altar, which was upon the altar of God. At which time according to the commandment they put to death certain women, that had caused their children to be circumcised. And they hanged the infants about their necks, and rifled their houses, and slew them that had circumcised them.

But many in Israel were fully resolved and confirmed in themselves not to eat any unclean thing. And they chose to die rather than they might not be defiled with meats, and that they might not profane the holy covenant: so then they died. And there was very great wrath upon Israel.

Chapter 2

In those days arose Mattathias, the son of John, the son of Simeon, a priest of the sons of Joarib, from Jerusalem, and dwelt in Modein. And he had five sons, Joannan, called Caddis; Simon, called Thassi; Judah, who was called Maccabee: Eleazar, called Avaran: and Jonathan, whose surname was Apphus.

And when he saw the blasphemies that were committed in Judaea and Jerusalem, he said, "Woe is me! wherefore was I born to see this misery of my people, and of the holy city, and to dwell there, when it was delivered into the hand of the enemy, and the sanctuary into the hand of strangers? Her temple is become as a man without glory. Her glorious vessels are carried away into captivity, her infants are slain in the streets, her young men with the sword of the enemy.

What nation hath not had a part in her kingdom, and gotten of her spoils? All her ornaments are taken away; of a free woman she is become a bondslave. And, behold, our sanctuary, even our beauty and our glory, is laid waste, and the Gentiles have profaned it. To what end therefore shall we live any longer?"

Then Mattathias and his sons rent their clothes, and put on sackcloth, and mourned greatly.

In the meanwhile the king's officers, such as compelled the people to revolt, came into the city Modein, to make them sacrifice. And when many of Israel came unto them, Mattathias also and his sons came together. Then spoke the king's officers to Mattathias, "You are a ruler, and an honorable and great man in this city, and strengthened with sons and brethren. Now therefore come first, and fulfill the king's commandment, like as all the Gentiles have done, yea, and the men of Judaea also, and such as remain in Jerusalem. Then shall you and your house be considered friends of the king, and you and your children shall be honored with silver and gold, and many rewards."

Then Mattathias answered and spoke with a loud voice, "Though all the nations that are under the king's dominion obey him, and fall away everyone from the religion of their fathers and give consent to his commandments, yet will I and my sons and my brethren walk in the covenant of our fathers. God forbid that we should forsake the law and the ordinances. We will not obey the king's commands to turn away from our religion, either on the right hand, or the left."

Now when he had finished speaking these words, there came one of the Jews in the sight of all to sacrifice on the altar which was at Modein, according to the king's commandment. When Mattathias saw him, he was inflamed with zeal, and his reins trembled, neither could he forbear to show his anger according to judgment. Therefore he ran and slew the traitor upon the altar. He killed also the king's commissioner, who compelled men to sacrifice, and pulled down the altar. Thus Mattathias dealt zealously for the law of God, like as Phinehas did unto Zimri the son of Salu.

And Mattathias cried throughout the city with a loud voice, saying, "Whosoever is zealous of the law and maintains the covenant, let him follow me." So he and his sons fled into the mountains, and left all that they had in the city.

Then many that sought after justice and judgment went into the wilderness to dwell there, both they, their children, their wives, and their cattle, because afflictions pressed heavily upon them. Now when it was told the king's servants and the host that were in Jerusalem, in the city of David, that certain men, who had broken the king's commandment, were gone down into hiding in the wilderness, the king's forces pursued them great number. And having caught up with them, they prepared to attack them and make war against them on the Sabbath day. And they said unto them, "Let that which you have done hitherto suffice, come forth, and do according to the commandment of the king, and you shall live." But they said, "We will not come forth, neither will we do the king's commandment, to profane the Sabbath day." So then the king's forces attacked immediately. But they answered them not, neither cast they a stone at them, nor defended the places where they lay hid, but said, "Let us die all in our innocence; heaven and earth shall testify for us, that you put us to death wrongfully." So they rose up against them in battle on the Sabbath and they slew them, with their wives and children, and their cattle, to the number of a thousand people.

Now when Mattathias and his friends learned of this, they mourned for them greatly. And one of them said to another, "If we all do as our brethren have done, and fight not for our lives and laws against the Gentiles, they will now quickly root us out of the earth." At that time therefore they decreed, saying, "Whosoever shall come to make battle with us on the Sabbath day, we will fight against him; neither will we die all, as our brethren that were murdered in the secret places."

Then came there unto him a company of Hassideans, who were mighty warriors of Israel, even all such as were voluntarily devoted unto the law. Also all they that fled for persecution joined them, and reinforced them. So they joined their forces, and struck down sinful men in their anger and wicked men in their wrath; but the rest fled to the Gentiles for safety. Then Mattathias and his friends went round about, and pulled down the altars; and what children they found within the coast of Israel uncircumcised, those they circumcised valiantly. They pursued also after the arrogant men, and the work prospered in their hands. So they recovered the law out of the hand of the Gentiles, and out of the hand of kings, neither suffered they the sinner to triumph.

Now when the time drew near that Mattathias should die, he said unto his sons, "Now hath pride and rebuke gotten strength, and the time of destruction and the wrath of indignation. Now therefore, my sons, be you zealous for the law, and give your lives for the covenant of your fathers.

"Call to remembrance what acts our fathers did in their time; so shall you receive great honor and an everlasting name. Was not Abraham found faithful when tested and it was reckoned to him as righteousness? Joseph in the time of his distress kept the commandment and was made lord of Egypt. Phinehas our ancestor in being zealous and fervent obtained the covenant of an everlasting priesthood. Joshua for fulfilling the word was made a judge in Israel. Caleb, for bearing witness before the congregation, received the heritage or the land. David, for being merciful, possessed the throne of an everlasting kingdom. Elijah for being zealous and fervent for the law, was taken up into heaven. Hananiah, Azariah, and Mishael, by believing, were saved out of the flame. Daniel, because of his innocence, was delivered from the mouth of lions.

"And thus consider you throughout all ages, that none that put their trust in him shall be overcome. Fear not then the words of a sinful man, for his glory shall be dung and worms. Today he shall be lifted up, and tomorrow he shall not be found, because he is returned into his dust, and his thought is come to nothing. Wherefore, you my sons, be valiant, and show yourselves men who follow the law, for by it shall you obtain glory.

"And, behold, I know that your brother Simon is a man of counsel, listen to him always, he shall be a father unto you. As for Judah Maccabee, he has been mighty and strong, even from his youth up, let him be your captain, and fight the battle of the people. Take also unto you all those that observe the law, and avenge the wrong of your people. Pay back the Gentiles, and obey the commandments of the law."

So he blessed them, and was gathered to his fathers. And he died in the hundred forty-sixth year, and his sons buried him in the sepulchers of his fathers at Modein, and all Israel made great lamentation for him.

Chapter 3

Then his son Judah, called Maccabee, rose up in his father's stead. And all his brethren helped him, and so did all they that held with his father, and they fought with cheerfulness the battle of Israel. So he gave his people great honor, and put on a breastplate as a giant, and girt his warlike harness about him, and he made battles protecting the host with his sword. In his acts he was like a lion, and like a lion's whelp roaring for his prey. For he pursued the wicked, and sought them out, and burned those that troubled his people. The wicked shrank for fear of him, and all the workers of iniquity were troubled, because salvation prospered in his hand. He grieved also many kings, and made Jacob glad with his acts, and his memorial is blessed forever. Moreover he went through the cities of Judaea, destroying the ungodly out of them, and turning away wrath from Israel. He was renowned to the ends of the earth, and he gathered in those who were perishing.

Then Apollonius gathered the Gentiles together and a great army out of Samaria to fight against Israel. When Judah learned of it, he went forth to meet him, and so defeated and killed him. Many also fell down slain, but the rest fled. They took their spoils, and Judah took Apollonius' sword, and he fought with it for the rest of his life.

When Seron, a prince of the army of Syria, heard that Judah had gathered a multitude of the faithful to go out with him to war, he said, "I will make a name for myself and win honor in the kingdom. I will fight with Judah and those that are with him who scorn the king's commandment." So he prepared a strong army of the ungodly about him to take vengeance upon the children of Israel.

And when he approached the ascent of Beth-horon, Judah went forth to meet him with a small company. When they saw the army coming to meet them, they said to Judah, "How shall we, being so few, be able to fight against so great and so strong a multitude, seeing we are ready to faint with fasting all this day?" Judah answered, "It is no hard matter for many to be shut up in the hands of a few; and with the God of heaven it is all one, to deliver a great multitude or a small company. For victory in battle depends not on the size of the army, but the strength that comes from heaven. They come against us with much pride and iniquity to destroy us and our wives and children, and to despoil us; but we fight for our lives and our laws. The Lord himself will overthrow them before our face; and as for you, be not afraid of them."

Now as soon as he had finished speaking, he leapt suddenly against Seron and his army, and they were overthrown. They pursued them down Beth-horon unto the plain where they killed eight hundred men; and the rest fled into the land of the Philistines.

Then began the fear of Judah and his brethren, and an exceeding great dread fell upon the nations round about them. His fame reached the king and all nations talked of the battles of Judah.

Now when king Antiochus heard these things, he was full of anger. He gathered together all the forces of his realm, a very strong army. He opened also his treasure and gave his soldiers pay for a year, commanding them to be ready whenever he should need them. Nevertheless, when he saw that the money in his treasury was exhausted and that the revenues from the country were small—because of the dissension and plague, which had been brought upon the land by taking away the laws which had existed from earliest times—he feared that he should not be able to bear the expense any longer, nor to have such gifts to give so liberally as he did before, for he used to give more liberally than preceding kings. Wherefore, being greatly perplexed in his mind, he determined to go into Persia, there to collect revenues from those countries and to gather much money.

So he left Lysias, a nobleman of royal blood, to oversee the affairs of the king from the river Euphrates unto the borders of Egypt. Lysias also was to bring up his son Antiochus, until he came back. Moreover he turned over half of his forces, and the elephants, and gave him charge of all things that he would have done. As concerning those that dwelt in Judaea and Jerusalem, he should send an army against them, to destroy and root out the strength of Israel, and the remnant of Jerusalem, and to take away tip their memorial from that place, and that he should settle aliens in all their territory, and divide their land by lot. So the king took half of the force that remained and departed from Antioch, his royal city, in the hundred and forty-seventh year he crossed the

Euphrates river and went through the high countries.

Then Lysias chose Ptolemy, the son of Dorymenes, and Nicanor and Gorgias, mighty men of the king's friends, and with them he sent forty thousand footmen and seven thousand horsemen to go into the land of Judaea, and to destroy it, as the king commanded. So they went forth with all their power, and came and pitched by Emmaus in the plain country. And the merchants of the country, hearing the fame of them, took silver and gold in immense amounts with servants, and came into the camp to buy the children of Israel for slaves. Also forces from Syria and of the land of the Philistines joined with them.

Now when Judah and his brothers saw that miseries were multiplied, and that the forces did encamp themselves on their borders. They knew also that the king had given commandment to destroy the people, and utterly abolish them. They said to each other, "Let us restore the ruins of our people, and let us fight for our people and the sanctuary." So then the congregation was gathered together that they might be ready for battle, and that they might pray and ask mercy and compassion. Now Jerusalem lay void as a wilderness, there was none of her children that went in or out. The sanctuary also was trodden down, and aliens kept the stronghold; the Gentiles had their habitation in that place. Joy was taken from Jacob, and the pipe with the harp ceased.

Then the Israelites assembled themselves together and came to Mizpah, opposite Jerusalem; because Israel formerly had a place of prayer in Mizpah. They fasted that day, and put on sackcloth and sprinkled ashes on their heads, and tore their clothes. And they opened the book of the law, wherein the Gentiles consulted the likenesses of their images. They brought also the priests' garments, and the first fruits, and the tithes, and the Nazarites they stirred up, who had accomplished their days. Then they cried with a loud voice toward heaven, saying, "What shall we do with these and whither shall we carry them away? For your sanctuary is trodden down and profaned, and your priests mourn in humiliation. And, lo, the Gentiles are assembled together against us to destroy us. What things they imagine against us, you know. How shall we be able to stand against them, except you, O God, with your help?"

They then sounded the trumpets, and cried with a loud voice. And after this Judah ordained captains over the people, even captains over thousands, and over hundreds, and over fifties, and over tens. Those who were building houses, or had betrothed wives, or were planting vineyards, or were fearful, those he commanded should return, every man to his own house, according to the law. So the camp removed, and pitched upon the south side of Emmaus.

And Judah said, "Arm yourselves, and be valiant men, and see that you be ready early in the morning to fight these Gentiles who have assembled together against us to destroy us and our sanctuary. It is better for us to die in battle than to see the misfortunes of our people and our sanctuary. Nevertheless, as the will of God is in heaven, so let him do."

Chapter 4

Now Gorgias took five thousand in infantry and one thousand picked cavalry, and this division moved out by night to fall upon the camp of the Jews and attack them suddenly. Men from the citadel were his guides. But Judah heard of it, and he and his warriors moved out to attack the king's force in Emmaus while the division was still absent from the camp. When Gorgias entered the camp of Judah by night, he found no one there, so he looked for them in the hills, because he said, "These men are running away from us."

At daybreak Judah appeared in the plain with three thousand men, but they did not have armor and swords such as they desired. And they saw the camp of the Gentiles, strong and fortified, with cavalry all around it; and these men were trained in war. But Judah said to those who were with him, "Do not fear their numbers or be afraid when they charge. Remember how our ancestors were saved at the Red Sea, when Pharaoh with his forces pursued them. And now, let us cry to Heaven, to see whether he will favor us and remember his covenant with our ancestors and crush this army before us today. Then all the Gentiles will know that there is one who redeems and saves Israel."

When the foreigners looked up and saw them coming against them, they went out from their camp to battle. Then the men with Judah blew their trumpets and engaged in battle. The Gentiles were crushed, and fled into the plain, and all those in the rear fell by the sword. They pursued them to Gazara, and to the plains of Idumea, and to Azotus and Jamnia; and three thousand of them fell. Then Judah and his force turned back from pursuing them, and he said to the people, "Do not be greedy for plunder, for there is a battle before us; Gorgias and his force are near us in the hills. But stand now against our enemies and fight them, and afterward seize the plunder boldly."

Just as Judah was finishing this speech, a detachment appeared, coming out of the hills. They saw that their army had been put to flight, and that the Jews were burning the camp, for the smoke that was seen showed what had happened. When they perceived this, they were greatly frightened, and when they also saw the army of Judah drawn up in the plain for battle, they all fled into the land of the Philistines. Then Judah returned to plunder the camp, and they seized a great amount of gold and silver, and cloth dyed blue and sea purple, and great riches. On their return they sang hymns and praises to Heaven—"For he is good, for his mercy endures forever." Thus Israel had a great deliverance that day.

Those of the foreigners who escaped went and reported to Lysias all that had happened. When he heard it, he was perplexed and discouraged, for things had not happened to Israel as he had intended, nor had they turned out as the king had ordered. But the next year he mustered sixty thousand picked infantry and five thousand cavalry to subdue them. They came into Idumea and encamped at Beth-zur, and Judah met them with ten thousand men.

When he saw that their army was strong, he prayed, saying, "Blessed are you, O Savior of Israel, who crushed the attack of the mighty warrior by the hand of your servant David, and gave the camp of the Philistines into the hands of Jonathan son of Saul, and of the man who carried his armor. Hem in this army by the hand of your people Israel, and let them be ashamed of their troops and their cavalry. Fill them with cowardice, melt the boldness of their strength; let them tremble in their destruction. Strike them down with the sword of those who love you, and let all who know your name praise you with hymns."

Then both sides attacked, and there fell of the army of Lysias five thousand men; they fell in action. When Lysias saw the rout of his troops and observed the boldness that inspired those of Judah, and how ready they were either to live or to die nobly, he withdrew to Antioch and enlisted mercenaries in order to invade Judaea again with an even larger army.

Then Judah and his brothers said, "See our enemies are crushed; let us go up to cleanse the sanctuary and dedicate it." So all the army assembled and went up to Mount Zion. There they saw the sanctuary desolate, the altar profaned, and the gates burned. In the courts they saw bushes sprung up as in a thicket, or as on one of the mountains. They saw also the chambers of the priests in ruins. Then they tore their clothes and mourned with great lamentation; they sprinkled themselves with ashes and fell face down on the ground. And when the signal was given with the trumpets, they cried out to Heaven.

Then Judah detailed men to fight against those in the citadel until he had cleansed the sanctuary. He chose blameless priests devoted to the law, and they cleansed the sanctuary and removed the defiled stones to an unclean place. They deliberated what to do about the altar of burnt offering, which had been profaned. And they thought it best to tear it down, so that it would not be a lasting shame to them that the Gentiles had defiled it. So they tore down the altar, and stored the stones in a convenient place on the temple hill until a prophet should come to tell what to do with them. Then they took unhewn stones, as the law directs, and built a new altar like the former one. They also rebuilt the sanctuary and the interior of the temple, and consecrated the courts. They made new holy vessels, and brought the lamp-stand, the altar of incense, and the table into the temple. Then they offered incense on the altar and lit the lamps on the lamp-stand, and these gave light in the temple. They placed the bread on the table and hung up the curtains. Thus they finished all the work they had undertaken.

Early in the morning on the twenty-fifth day of the ninth month, which is the month of Kislev, in the one hundred forty-eighth year, they rose and offered sacrifice, as the law directs, on the new altar of burnt offering that they had built. At the very season and on the very day that the Gentiles had profaned it, it was dedicated with songs and harps and lutes and cymbals. All the people fell on their faces and worshipped and blessed Heaven, who had prospered them. So they celebrated the dedication of the altar for eight days, and joyfully offered burnt offerings; they offered a sacrifice of well-being and a thanksgiving offering. They decorated the front of the temple with golden crowns and small shields; they restored the gates and the chambers for the priests, and fitted them with doors. There was very great joy among the people, and the disgrace brought by the Gentiles was removed.

Then Judah and his brothers and all the assembly of Israel determined that every year at that season the days of dedication of the altar should be observed with joy and gladness for eight days, beginning with the twenty-fifth day of the month of Kislev.

From

The Second Book of Maccabees

The Martyrdom of Eleazar

Eleazar, one of the scribes in high position, a man now advanced in age and of noble presence, was being forced to open his mouth to eat swine's flesh.

But he, welcoming death with honor rather than life with pollution, went up to the rack of his own accord, spitting out the flesh, as all ought to go who have the courage to refuse things that it is not right to taste, even for the natural love of life.

Those who were in charge of that unlawful sacrifice took the man aside because of their long acquaintance with him, and privately urged him to bring meat of his own providing, proper for him to use, and to pretend that he was eating the flesh of the sacrificial meal that had been commanded by the king, so that by doing this he might be saved from death, and be treated kindly on account of his old friendship with them. But making a high resolve, worthy of his years and the dignity of his old age and the gray hairs that he had reached with distinction and his excellent life even from childhood, and moreover according to the holy God-given law, he declared himself quickly, telling them to send him to Hades.

"Such pretense is not worthy of our time of life," he said, "for many of the young might suppose that Eleazar in his ninetieth year had gone over to an alien religion, and through my pretense, for the sake of living a brief moment longer, they would be led astray because of me, while I defile and disgrace my old age. Even if for the present I would avoid the punishment of mortals, yet whether I live or die I will not escape the hands of the Almighty. Therefore, by bravely giving up my life now, I will show myself worthy of my old age and leave to the young a noble example of how to die a good death willingly and nobly for the revered and holy laws."

When he had said this, he went at once to the rack. Those who a little before had acted toward him with goodwill now changed to ill will, because the words he had uttered were in their opinion sheer madness. When he was about to die under the blows, he groaned aloud and said: "It is dear to the Lord in his holy knowledge that, though I might have been saved from death, I am enduring terrible sufferings in my body under this beating, but in my soul I am glad to suffer these things because I fear him."

So in this way he died, leaving in his death an example of nobility and a memorial of courage, not only to the young but to the great body of his nation.

2 MACCABEES 6:18–31

The Seven Brothers and Their Mother

It happened also that seven brothers and their mother were arrested and were being compelled by the king, under torture with whips and thongs, to partake of unlawful swine's flesh. One of them, acting as their spokesman, said, "What do you intend to ask and learn from us? For we are ready to die rather than transgress the laws of our ancestors."

The king fell into a rage, and gave orders to have pans and caldrons heated. These were heated immediately, and he commanded that the tongue of their spokesman be cut out and that they scalp him and cut off his hands and feet, while the rest of the brothers and the mother looked on. When he was utterly helpless, the king ordered them to take him to the fire, still breathing, and to fry him in a pan. The smoke from the pan spread widely, but the brothers and their mother encouraged one another to die nobly, saying, "The Lord God is watching over us and in truth has compassion on us, as Moses declared in his song that bore witness against the people to their faces, when he said, 'And he will have compassion on his servants.'"

After the first brother had died in this way, they brought forward the second for their sport. They tore off the skin of his head with the hair, and asked him, "Will you eat rather than have your body punished limb by limb?" He replied in the language of his ancestors and said to them, "No." Therefore he in turn underwent tortures as the first brother had done. And when he was at his last breath, he said, "You accursed wretch, you dismiss us from this present life, but the King of the universe will raise us up to an everlasting renewal of life, because we have died for his laws."

After him, the third was the victim of their sport. When it was demanded, he quickly put out his tongue and courageously stretched forth his hands. He said nobly, "I got these from Heaven, and because of his laws I disdain them, and from him I hope to get them back again." As a result the king himself and those with him were astonished at the young man's spirit, for he regarded his sufferings as nothing.

After he too had died, they maltreated and tortured the fourth in the same way. When he was near death, he said, "One cannot but choose to die at the hands of mortals and to cherish the hope God gives of being raised again by him. But for you there will be no resurrection to life!"

Next they brought forward the fifth and maltreated him. But he looked at the king, and said, "Because you have authority among mortals, though you also are mortal, you do what you please.

But do not think that God has forsaken our people. Keep on, and see how his mighty power will torture you and your descendants!"

After him they brought forward the sixth. And when he was about to die, he said, "Do not deceive yourself in vain. For we are suffering these things on our own account, because of our sins against our own God. Therefore astounding things have happened. But do not think that you will go unpunished for having tried to fight against God!"

The mother was especially admirable and worthy of honorable memory. Although she saw her seven sons perish within a single day, she bore it with good courage because of her hope in the Lord. She encouraged each of them in the language of their ancestors. Filled with a noble spirit, she reinforced her woman's reasoning with a man's courage, and said to them, "I do not know how you came into being in my womb. It was not I who gave you life and breath, nor I who set in order the elements within each of you. Therefore the Creator of the world, who shaped the beginning of humankind and devised the origin of all things, will in his mercy give life and breath back to you again, since you now forget yourselves for the sake of his laws."

Antiochus felt that he was being treated with contempt, and he was suspicious of her reproachful tone. The youngest brother being still alive, Antiochus not only appealed to him in words, but promised with oaths that he would make him rich and enviable if he would turn from the ways of his ancestors, and that he would take him for his friend and entrust him with public affairs. Since the young man would not listen to him at all, the king called the mother to him and urged her to advise the youth to save himself. After much urging on his part, she undertook to persuade her son. But, leaning close to him, she spoke in their native language as follows, deriding the cruel tyrant: "My son, have pity on me. I carried you nine months in my womb, and nursed you for three years and have reared you and brought you up to this point in your life, and have taken care of you. I beg you, my child, to look at the heaven and the earth and see everything that is in them, and recognize that God did not make them out of things that existed. And in the same way the human race came into being. Do not fear this butcher, but prove worthy of your brothers. Accept death so that in God's mercy I may get you back again along with your brothers."

While she was still speaking, the young man said, "What are you waiting for? I will not obey the king's command, but I obey the command of the law that was given to our ancestors through Moses. But you who have contrived all sorts of evil against the Hebrews, will certainly not escape the hands of God. For we are suffering because of our own sins. And if our living Lord is angry for a little while, to rebuke and discipline us, he will again be reconciled with his own servants. But you unholy wretch, you most defiled of all mortals, do not be elated in vain and puffed up by uncertain hopes, when you raise your hand against the children of Heaven. You have not yet escaped the judgment of the almighty, all-seeing God. For our brothers after enduring a brief suffering have drunk of ever-flowing life, under God's covenant; but you by the judgment of God, will receive just punishment for your arrogance. I, like my brothers, give up body and life for the laws of our ancestors, appealing to God to show mercy soon to our nation and by trials and plagues to make you confess that he alone is God, and through me and my brothers to bring to an end the wrath of the Almighty that has justly fallen on our whole nation."

The king fell into a rage, and handled him worse than the others, being exasperated at his scorn. So he died in his integrity, putting his whole trust in the Lord.

Last of all, the mother died, after her sons.

Let this be enough, then, about the eating of sacrifices and the extreme tortures.

2 MACCABEES 7

The
Hanukkah
Celebration

Candlelighting

The major ritual act of Hanukkah is the kindling of lights. These lights are a reminder of the miracle of Hanukkah. As told in the First Book of Maccabees, Judah rekindled the Temple menorah after cleansing it, and the practice of candlelighting became central to the Hanukkah holiday.

Why are there eight lights? Some Jewish scholars believe that the Hanukkah rededication of the Temple celebration followed after the original eight-day dedication of Solomon's Temple. However, the most popular legend explaining the eight lights is the single jug of oil that miraculously lasted eight days instead of just one, recorded in the Talmud:

> What is the reason for Hanukkah? For our Rabbis taught: On the twenty-fifth of Kislev begin the days of Hanukkah, which are eight on which a lamentation for the dead and fasting are forbidden. For when the Greeks entered the Temple, they defiled all the oils therein, and when the Hasmonean dynasty prevailed against and defeated them, they searched and found only one cruse of oil which had the seal of the high priest, but which contained only enough oil for one day's lighting only; yet a miracle happened and they lit the

lamp which remained lit for eight days. The following year these days were appointed a festival with the recital of Hallel and thanksgiving.

SHABBAT 21B

In many peoples' minds, there is confusion between the seven-branched menorah and the nine-branched lamp, the *hanukkiah*, which is used during the Hanukkah celebration. These are two religiously significant and different Jewish candelabra. The seven-branched menorah, with its tree-like form, was probably a representation of the Tree of Life in the Garden of Eden (its seven branches were also believed to represent the seven days of creation with). The menorah is the more ancient of the two, and was used in Solomon's Temple. When Judah and his men rededicated the Temple, the lamp they lit was a seven-branched menorah.

But it is forbidden to reproduce the Temple menorah and it was not until the Middle Ages that menorah-forms of Hanukkah lamps were made. Since the Hanukkah lamp had nine branches and the size, material, and decoration were different from the original Temple menorah, it was no longer considered a violation to make *hanukkiot* of the menorah type. There is confusion today because the word "menorah" is often used as a general term to identify either lamp.

The major difference between the Temple menorah and the *hanukkiah* is the number of branches—

the menorah of the Temple had seven branches, while the later *hanukkiah* has nine. Most early Hanukkah lamps burned olive oil and were made from either stone or metal and were originally meant to be placed outside the entrance of the household.

While eight lights are required on the *hanukkiah*, one to be lit each night of Hanukkah, it became customary for the Hanukkah lamp to have a place for nine flames. The ninth flame is called the *shamash* ("the servant"), since its purpose is to light the others. The reason for the *shamash* comes from the Jewish religious prohibition that states that the Hanukkah lights themselves cannot serve any pragmatic purpose other than to "publicize the miracle." All candles should be of the same height, although the *shamash* is usually positioned higher—it can also be lower—to distinguish it from the other eight candles.

While the *hanukkiah* was originally put outdoors, the common practice today is to place it on a window sill. Other locations can be such convenient central areas in the home as the fireplace mantle or the dining room table. The *hanukkiah* should not be moved after the lights are kindled, although it can be repositioned from night to night.

The placement of the candles in the *hanukkiah* and the proper procedure for kindling the lights is *set to the left*, while you *light to the right*. First set the *shamash* in its holder, and place the first night's candle in the far right holder. On the second night, add a candle in the next holder toward the left of the first night's candle. And on the following nights, continue to add one candle toward the left until all holders are filled on the eighth night.

The order for kindling the lights is to light the *shamash,* and then the most recently added candle is lit first.

Every Hanukkah includes at least one Shabbat, and the Hanukkah lights are kindled before lighting the Sabbath candles on Friday night. If Havdalah—the ceremony connoting the differentiation between the holiness of the Sabbath day and the ordinary days of the week—is said at home, it precedes the lighting of the Hanukkah candles. The candles are to be lit any time after sunset, usually before sitting down to dinner.

The Hanukkah ritual has a fixed order of blessings and actions. Each blessing and each prayer in the Hanukkah candlelighting service has a purpose and a function in bringing the experience of the celebration alive. There are three blessings (*b'rakhot*) on the first night (two on the next seven nights) and then songs or prayers.

After the *shammash* is lit, the blessings are recited.

The first blessing is:

> Blessed art Thou, Lord our God, Ruler of the universe, who has sanctified us with Thy commandments and has commanded us to kindle the Hanukkah light.

The second blessing is:

Blessed art Thou, Lord, our God, Ruler of the universe, who did perform miracles for our fathers in those days at this season.

The third blessing, which is said only on the *first* night, is:

Blessed art Thou, Lord our God, Ruler of the universe, who hast granted us life, and sustained us, and brought us to this season.

Then the newest candle is lit first. After all the candles on that particular night of Hanukkah are lit, the *shammash* is placed back in its holder.

Then the *Ha-neirot Hallalu* is recited. It is a short traditional prayer to be said while the *hanukkiah* is burning. It is a one-paragraph authorized explanation of the Hanukkah story in which a review of all the key points found in the Talmud are expressed. The *Ha-neirot Hallalu* was created by rabbinic scholars around 700 C.E.

We kindle these lights to commemorate the miracles and the wonders, and the victorious battles that our ancestors accomplished in those days at this season through the hands of Your holy priests. During all the eight days of Hanukkah these lights are sanctified, and we are not permitted to make use of them except to look at them, in order to give thanks and to praise Your Name for Your miracles, Your wonders, and Your deliverance.

The Sephardim (Jews from Spanish and Arabic-speaking countries) also recite Psalm 30, attributed to King David, which is also called "A Song at the Dedication of the House." It has been suggested that it was sung by Judah and his men when they rededicated the Temple. Ashkenazim do not recite it at home but at synagogue services for Hanukkah.

"Maoz Tzur" ("Rock of Ages") is usually sung by Ashkenazim (Jews from East European ancestry) immediately after the candle-lighting ceremony. It is the most famous of all Hanukkah songs. The words of this hymn were composed by a man named Mordecai in the Middle Ages over six hundred years ago. He "signed" his work by forming an acrostic using the letters of his name to begin each verse of the first five stanzas. The original music was different from what is used now, which is a combination of a sixteenth-century German church hymn and a German folk song.

The first stanza of the song goes:

> Mighty, praised beyond compare,
>   Rock of my salvation,
> Build again my house of prayer,
>   For Thy habitation!
> Offering and libation, shall a ransomed nation
>   Joyful bring
>   There, and sing
> Psalms of dedication!

Al ha-Nissim

In the Grace After Meals—*Birkat ha-Mazon*—as well as in the *Amidah* (the Eighteen Benedictions, recited silently while standing at the central prayer of the three daily prayer services) an additional prayer, *Al ha-Nissim,* is recited throughout the eight days of Hanukkah. It is a reminder of thanksgiving and divine intervention and deliverance from the enemy. It epitomizes the Maccabean struggle, emphasizing the spiritual aspect over the military.

> We thank You for the miracles and for the redemptions and for the mighty deeds and for the deliverance and for the victorious battles that you waged for our fathers' ancestors in those days at this season.
>
> In the days of Mattathias son of Joannan, the High Priest, the Hasmonean and his sons, arose the kingdom of the wicked Greek government against Your people Israel trying to force them to abandon Your Torah and violate Your laws. And You in Your great mercy stood by them in their time of travail. You redeemed them, You defended them, You avenged their

wrongs. You delivered the strong into the hands of the weak, the many into the hands of the few, the corrupt into the hands of the pure, the guilty into the hands of the innocent, and the arrogant into the hands of those faithful to your Torah. And You achieved a great name and Your holiness is revealed to the world. For Your people Israel You wrought a great deliverance and a triumph on this day. And after this Your children came to Your Holy of Holies, Your Temple, and to cleanse Your sanctuary and to purify Your Holy altar and to kindle lights in Your sacred courtyards. And they established these eight days of Hanukkah to give thanks and to praise Your great name.

Games and Gifts

From the earliest days of the holiday, games have been a customary part of the Hanukkah celebration. Some scholars believe that games of luck played reflect the "luck" of the victorious Maccabees.

The most popular Hanukkah game is a one played with a spinning top called a *dreidel,* in yiddish, or *s'vivon,* in Hebrew. The familiar four-sided dreidel became widespread as a Hanukkah amusement among Ashkenazic Jews at the beginning of the Middle Ages.

There is a Hebrew letter on each of the dreidel's four sides: נ (*nun*), ג (*gimel*), ה (*he*), שׁ (*shin*). They stand for Yiddish words meaning "take" (*rem*) or "nothing" (*nisht*), "give" (*gib*) or "all" (*gantz*), "half" (*halb*), and "put" (*shtel*). The letters are interpreted to stand for the initial letters of the phrase *Nes gadol haya sham* ("a great miracle happened there"), referring to the miracle of Hanukkah that took place in Israel. Dreidels made in Israel replace the letter שׁ (*shin*) with פ (*pey*); the substitution means "a great miracle happened here," meaning Israel.

Children play the game by betting nuts or candy to the "pot." Then each child spins the dreidel in turn. Depending on which letter is showing when the top lands determines the reward or loss. If the player spins נ (*nun*), "nothing" (*nisht*), nothing happens and he passes; ג (*gimel*) means the player gets all that is in the "pot" (in which case everybody contributes to make up a new "pot"); ה (*he*) means the player gets one-half of the "pot"; שׁ (*shin*) means the player must put into the "pot" whatever amount was agreed upon when the game began. The game ends when one player has won everything from the others.

Another form of the game makes use of the numerical values of the letters: *nun*= 50, *gimel*= 3, *he*= 5, *shin*= 300.

Other games that are played are chess, with the

opposing sides representing the Maccabees and the Syrian-Greeks, and cards.

It is customary to give presents on Hanukkah, mainly to children, who usually receive Hanukkah *gelt* (Yiddish for "money") in the form of savings bonds, checks, or chocolate coins wrapped in gold foil. Giving gifts on Hanukkah is not, as is sometimes implied, merely imitative of Christmas.

Hanukkah
Recipes

Potato Latkes

Latkes, or potato pancakes, have become the quintessential culinary symbol of Hanukkah, even though they are a relatively new addition to Jewish cuisine. The potato was discovered in South America by early explorers in the sixteenth century. Because potato latkes are fried in oil, they symbolize the miracle of the cruse of oil that lasted eight days. Makes about 30 three-inch potato pancakes.

$2\frac{1}{2}$ *pounds potatoes, preferably baking potatoes, peeled*

1 *large onion*

3 *large eggs, lightly beaten*

1 *teaspoon salt, or to taste*

$\frac{1}{8}$ *teaspoon black pepper, or to taste*

2–3 *tablespoons all-purpose white flour, preferably unbleached*
Vegetable oil for frying
Applesauce, sour cream, or plain yogurt to serve

Shred the potatoes alternately with the onion to keep the potatoes from darkening. Squeeze the excess moisture from the potato and onion shreds. Mix in the eggs, salt, pepper, and matzo meal. Let the mixture rest for about 5 minutes. If the mixture still seems very wet, add a bit more flour.

In a very large skillet, over medium-high heat, heat oil that is about $\frac{1}{8}$ to $\frac{1}{4}$ inch deep until very hot. Use a large spoon to transfer some of the potato mixture to the oil, then flatten the mixture slightly with the back of the spoon to form a latke.

Continue until the skillet is full and fry the latkes until they are browned on both sides and crisp around the edges. Drain them well on paper towels. Repeat the process until all the latkes are fried.

Serve the latkes as soon as possible for the best taste and accompany them with applesauce, sour cream, or yogurt.

Loukoumades

Loukoumades, or fried honey puffs, are a traditional Hanukkah treat for Sephardic Jews who come from Greece and Turkey. Makes about 36 honey puffs.

Batter

- 2¼ teaspoons active dry yeast
- 1 cup warm (105 to 115 degrees) water
- ½ teaspoon sugar
- 1 large egg
- 2 cups all-purpose white flour, unbleached
- ¼ teaspoon salt

Honey Syrup

- 1 cup sugar
- ¾ cup cold water
- ½ cup honey
- 1 tablespoon lemon juice

Vegetable oil for frying
Ground cinnamon for garnish

For the batter: in a medium-sized bowl mix together the yeast, ½ cup of the warm water, and the sugar. Leave yeast mixture for 5 minutes, or until foamy. Stir in the remaining batter ingredients—including the remaining ½ cup of water—until smooth; it should be loose and sticky. Cover the bowl with plastic wrap and let the batter rise for 1 hour.

In the meantime prepare the honey syrup. Mix together all the ingredients in a saucepan and, over medium-high heat, slowly bring to a boil. Stir until the sugar dissolves and then lower the heat slightly and boil the syrup, uncovered, for five minutes. Remove from the heat and cool at room temperature.

After the batter has risen, stir it down. Put enough oil into a large saucepan so that it is about 1½ inches deep and heat until very hot, about 375 degrees. Use a spoon to scoop a small portion of the batter and gently drop into the oil. The batter will puff up to almost twice its original size. Repeat procedure, but do not overcrowd the pan. Fry the puffs, and using a slotted spoon turn them occasionally until they are browned on all sides and crisp.

Drain puffs on paper towels and then drop one or two at a time into the cooled syrup. Use tongs to turn the puffs in the syrup until coated. Let the excess syrup drain off; place puffs on a plate. Repeat until all the batter is used. Then sprinkle the puffs with cinnamon.

Soofganiyot

In Israel, *soofganiyot,* or jelly doughnuts, are the favorite treat eaten during Hanukkah. Makes 12 doughnuts.

Dough
- 4½ *teaspoons active dry yeast*
- 1 *cup warm (105 to 115 degrees) water*
- ⅓ *cup plus 1 teaspoon granulated sugar, divided*
- ⅓ *cup butter, melted and cooled*

1 *large egg*
1 *large egg yolk (reserve the white)*
1 *teaspoon salt*
$\frac{1}{4}$ *cup instant nonfat dry milk powder*
$3\frac{1}{3}$ *cups all-purpose white flour, unbleached*

Filling
  $\frac{1}{4}$ *cup thick jam*

  Vegetable oil for frying
  Granulated or confectioner's sugar for
  coating

Combine the yeast, $\frac{1}{2}$ cup of the water, and 1 teaspoon sugar in a large mixing bowl. Leave mixture for five minutes, or until foamy, and then add the remaining $\frac{1}{2}$ cup water, the $\frac{1}{3}$ cup sugar, melted butter, egg, egg yolk, salt, instant nonfat dry milk, and $2\frac{1}{3}$ cups of the flour. Beat with an electric mixer at medium speed for 3 minutes and then stir in the remaining 1 cup flour by hand to make a soft dough.

Cover the bowl with plastic wrap and a dish towel and let the dough rise in a warm place for about 1 to $1\frac{1}{2}$ hours, or until doubled in bulk.

On a lightly floured surface turn the dough out and knead it for about 2 minutes, or until smooth. Let the dough rest for 10 minutes and then divide in half, and roll out each half to a $\frac{1}{4}$-inch thickness. Cut out twelve three-inch-diameter circles from each half.

Beat the reserved egg white until frothy and

brush over one of the circles. Place a very small tea-spoon of jam in the center of the circle and top it with another circle, like a sandwich. Pinch the outside edges of the circles together to seal tightly. Place on a floured baking sheet or board. Repeat with remaining circles and jam. Cover the doughnuts loosely with a dish towel and allow them to rise for one hour.

Pour enough oil into a large saucepan so that it is about 2 inches deep and heat until hot, about 350 degrees. Drop a few doughnuts into the oil and fry them until they are puffed and golden brown, about 3 minutes on each side. Drain doughnuts on paper towels and then coat them while warm with granulated or confectioner's sugar. Repeat until all twelve of the doughnuts have been fried and coated.

Sukariyot Soomsoom

Sukariyot soomsoom, or crunchy sesame seed candy, is very popular among Sephardic families at Hanukkah time. It originated in ancient times and is made by Jews from the Middle East and North Africa. Makes about 64 small candies.

> *Vegetable oil or non-stick cooking spray for the pan*
> 2 *cups sesame seeds (about 12 ounces)*
> $\frac{1}{2}$ *cup honey*

$\frac{1}{2}$ *cup packed dark or light brown sugar*
$\frac{1}{2}$ *teaspoon ground cinnamon*
$\frac{1}{4}$ *teaspoon ground ginger*

Coat a 9-inch-square baking pan or dish with oil or non-stick cooking spray.

Put the sesame seeds in an ungreased 10-inch skillet and stir them over medium-high heat for five to ten minutes, or until they are lightly browned. Temporarily transfer the seeds to a bowl, making sure that none are left in the skillet, and set aside.

Mix the honey, brown sugar, cinnamon, and ginger in the skillet and slowly bring the mixture to a boil over medium heat, stirring constantly. When the mixture comes to a full boil, cook it vigorously for exactly 2 minutes. Remove the skillet from the heat and stir in the sesame seeds. Pour the hot mixture into the prepared pan. With a metal spatula that has been dipped into cold water, press the candy into a very smooth and even layer.

Cool the candy in the pan for 15 minutes, or until it is lukewarm. Loosen the candy by running the spatula around the edge of the pan and turn out the whole slab of candy onto a cutting surface. With a sharp knife cut the warm candy into very small squares, diamonds, or rectangles.

Allow the the candies to cool completely and then store in an airtight container at room temperature.